FARM CHARM

In the FARMHOUSE

by Pearl Markovics

Consultant:
Beth Gambro
Reading Specialist
Yorkville, Illinois

Contents

BEARPORT PUBLISHING

New York, New York

In the Farmhouse

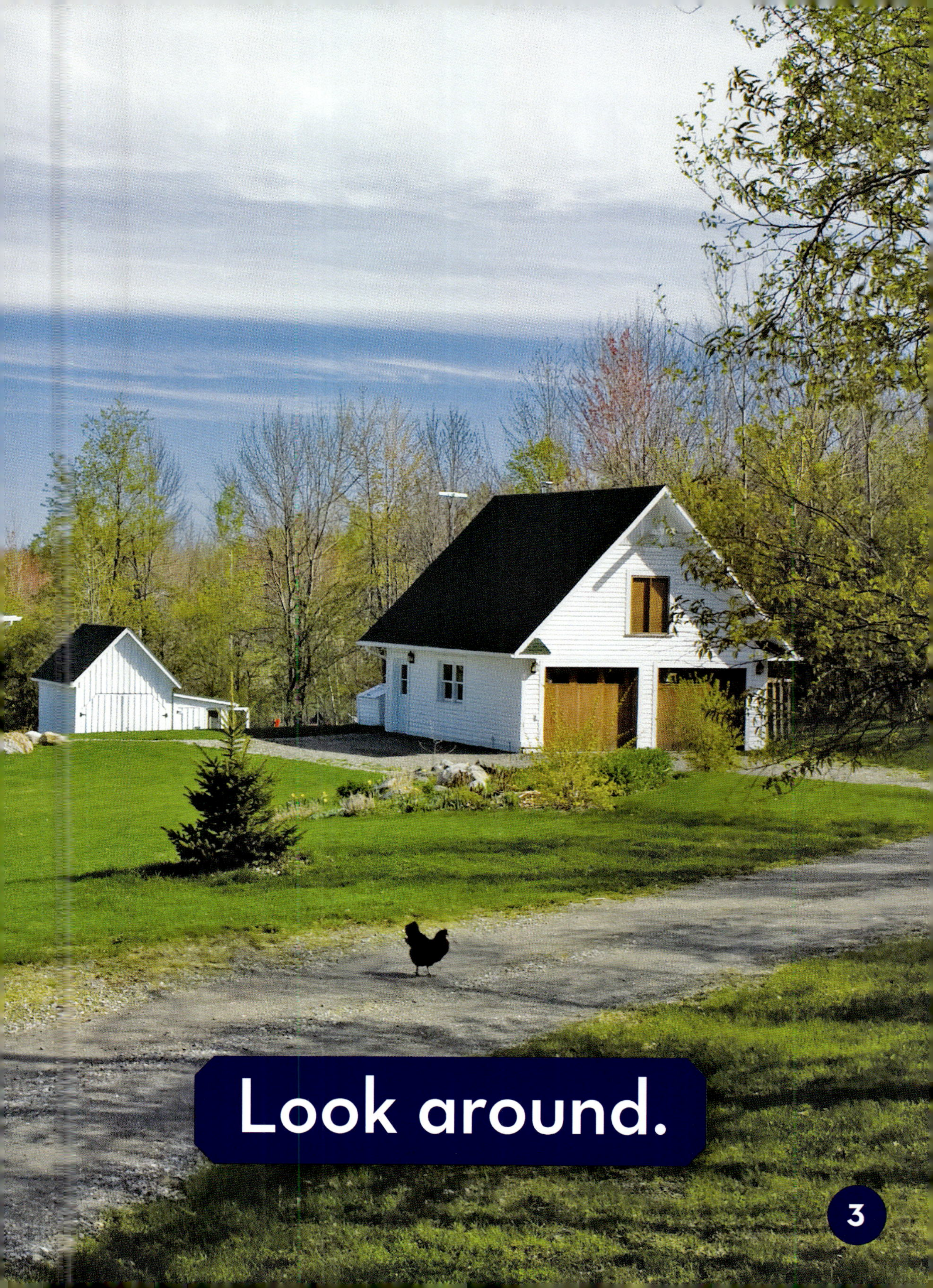

Look around.

What do you see?

I see a chair in the farmhouse.

What do you see?

I see a dog in the farmhouse.

What do you see?

I see a pie in the farmhouse.

Yum!

What do you see?

I see a sink in the farmhouse.

What do you see?

I see a bed in the farmhouse.

Look closely!

What do you see
in the farmhouse?

Key Words

bed

chair

dog

pie

sink

Index

About the Author

Pearl Markovics grew up on a small farm in New York. She loves sitting on the big front porch of her home.